MASTERCHEF FOOD PROCESSORS

SUCCESSFUL COOKING

Christine & Bernard Charretton

TELECUISINE

CONTENTS

Photos: Hervé Amiard
Graphic design: Michèle Fraudreau
Illustrations: Pascale Etchecopar

INTRODUCTION

Remember R2 D2, the clever little robot in « Star Wars »?
Well, your MASTERCHEF has just as many tricks to offer.
Welcome to « Star Cooking »!

Your Masterchef will make cooking painless. Have you already tried
kneading dough or chou pastry by hand? If you have, you'll know
how much "elbow grease" it takes. With your Masterchef, it will be
ready in a few seconds, so all you have to think about is how best to
eat it.

Your Masterchef food processor's accessories will make life so
much easier by helping you to prepare your food with maximum
efficiency. To get the most out of your processor, keep it close at
hand. While you are going through this booklet, you will discover that
it does more than just grate carrots, blend soups and beat
mayonnaises. It can also chop, fine chop, slice, mash, grind, beat,
knead, mix, whisk, extract juices, squeeze, pulp, sift, etc. It will free
you from all those time-consuming, difficult and boring tasks so that
you can concentrate on getting all your dishes just right.

We have tried out over 80 recipes, from aperitifs right through to
desserts for every day or special occasions, to help you get the most
out of your processor. And we have also given you some extra hints
so that you can use your imagination to vary a lot of the recipes to
create your own dishes.

SUCCESSFUL COOKING is that much easier with MASTERCHEF.

ACCESSORIES

Most of the accessories in the table below come with your food processor, but others are optional. The table is designed to help you choose the right accessory for what you need to prepare. You will find that you can sometimes use different accessories to perform the same task. You can be sure that whatever processor model you have chosen, once you have got used to it, it will do absolutely everything!

METAL BLADE	GRATING/SLICING DISC A/D fine grating/slicing	A/D
PLASTIC BLADE	GRATING/SLICING DISC C/H coarse grating/slicing	C/H
METAL KNEADING BLADE	SLICING DISC Chips	E
BLENDER ATTACHMENT	WHISK ATTACHMENT	
MILL	JUICE EXTRACTOR	
MASTERPRESS	CITRUS PRESS ATTACHMENT	

AND FUNCTIONS

CHOPPING Meat, fish, vegetables, fruit, cheese, dried fruits, chocolate, etc.	**SLICING** Potatoes (chips), vegetable sticks E
FINE CHOPPING Garlic, onion, mixed herbs, ham, bread	**KNEADING** Cake, pastries, shortcrust pastry, etc.
BLENDING Soups, compotes, drinks	**MIXING** Pancake, waffle, doughnut mixtures
LIQUIDIZING Soups, veloutés, creams, milk shake	**BEATING • WHISKING WHIPPING** Mayonnaise, light sauces, whipped cream, chantilly
MASHING Potatoes, fresch vegetables, fruit	**JUICE EXTRACTOR** Fruit and vegetables
GRATING Vegetables, fruit, cheese C/A	**SQUEEZING CITRUS FRUITS** Lemons, oranges, grapefruit
SLICING Vegetables, fruit D/H	**PUREEING** Tomatoes, fruit

CHOPPING

1. Cut the food to be chopped into small pieces. You can chop up to 600 g of meat (first removing any sinews), raw or cooked fish, vegetables, cheese, etc. Set the speed to MAX.

2. Chop for 15 to 20 seconds. For finer chopping, increase the time until you get the right texture. For coarse chopping use the « PULSE » button.

3. To chop dried fruit or chocolate, etc., set the speed to MAX. If you want to grind your dried fruit, chop in short bursts for best results: "PULSE".

4. Increase or decrease the chopping time depending on whether you want to chop coarsely or finely.

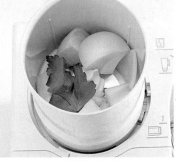

5. Use the mill for chopping small quantities. Chop an onion and add mixed herbs.

6. Make sure the herbs are dry before chopping. Set the speed to MAX and chop for 20 seconds. Do the same for fruit peel, spices or dried fruits (up to 50 g).

BLENDING

1. You can blend up to 1 litre of soup or compote. Dice and cook the vegetables then put them with their cooking water into the bowl fitted with the metal blade.

2. Set the speed to MIN and turn gradually up to MAX. Blend for 20 seconds for soups.

3. Use the blender attachment for blending and liquidizing. Pour liquids in first, then solids.

4. Set the speed to MIN and turn up gradually to MAX. You can do this for making milkshakes, drinks, creamed soups, pancake mixture, etc.

MASHING-PUREEING

1. Fit on the masterpress attachment with the wide-mesh sieve. Set the speed to 3 and switch on. Feed in diced cooked potatoes through the feeder tube.

2. Add a little cooking water towards the end. Choose the appropriate sieve, small, medium or wide-mesh, for your recipe : purée, sauce or juice.

3. Use the metal blade for pureeing stewed fruit. Leave stewed fruit to drain then put in the bowl. Set to speed 3 and blend.

4. Turn the speed up gradually to 12. You can puree carrots, celery, etc. Potatoes stick to the blade, use the masterpress.

5. You can use the mill to puree up to 100 g of food for your baby. Put cooked vegetables in the mill, adding a little meat, ham or fish, to taste.

6. Set the speed to MAX and use the « PULSE » button for best results.
Please refer to individual recipes for alternative accessory according to the model you have chosen.

GRATING · SLICING · MAKING CHIPS

A/D

1. Use side A of the disk to grate carrots or cheese finely, and side D for fine slices of cucumber, radishes, etc. Feed in horizontally through the feeder tube...

2. ...to obtain long slivers or slices. Set the speed to MAX. Use the pusher to push food down the feeder tube.

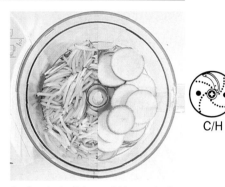

C/H

3. Use side C to coarsely grate courgettes, beetroots, apples, etc., and side H to cut thick slices. Feed in vertically...

4. ...for short sticks or thick round slices. Depending on the amount or size of the food to be processed, use the small or large feeder tube.

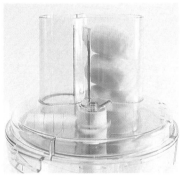

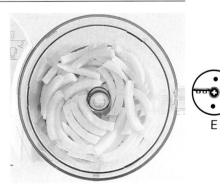

E

5. Use disk E for making chips. Peel the potatoes and lie them flat in the feeder tube.

6. Set the speed to MAX and switch on. You can prepare up to 1 kg of ingredients at a time.

KNEADING

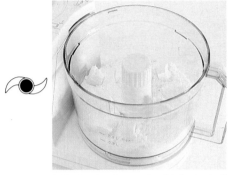

1. Shortcrust pastry: pour flour into bowl and add salt and knobs of butter. Set the speed to 4 and switch on for 10 seconds.

4. Dough: pour flour into the bowl and add yeast and salt. Set the speed to 6 and press « PULSE » button 4 times. Pour in water through the feeder tube.

2. Pour in the water through the feeder tube with the blender still running (15 seconds).

5. Knead for 20 seconds and turn the speed up to 12; then continue kneading for 1 min 15 sec. to obtain a smooth, supple texture.

3. Turn up to speed 8 for 15 seconds until the pastry has rolled into a ball.

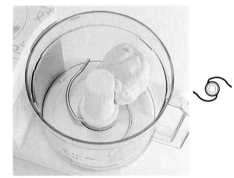

6. You can fit a metal kneading blade on 680 models. This can be used instead of the plastic kneading blade for heavy shortcrust and shortbread (sablé) pastries and doughs or light pound cake or sponge mixtures, etc.

MIXING

1. Pound cake: use the plastic kneading blade for a light mixture. Mix in the eggs and sugar.

2. Add the flour and soft knobs of butter. Set the speed to 3...

3. ...then turn up gradually to 12 to obtain a smooth and even mixture.

4. Pancake mixture: set the speed to MIN. Pour the milk into the bowl, then add the flour, egg, butter and flavouring.

BEATING · WHISKING

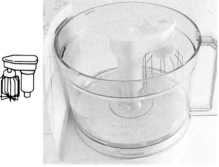

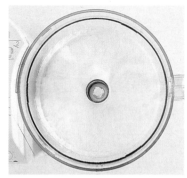

1. Stiffly beaten egg whites: pour the egg whites (2 to 6) into the bowl, add a pinch of salt and set the speed to MAX.

2. Switch on and beat the whites until stiff (1 min 30 to 2 min.).

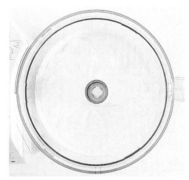

3. Whipped cream: pour well chilled cream into the bowl (leave for a few minutes beforehand in the freezer), set the speed to 3 and switch on.

4. Gradually turn the speed up to 12. Stop once you can see that the cream has a firm consistency (the time required will vary with the quantity).

5. Mayonnaise: Put the egg, mustard and salt in the bowl. Set the speed to 3 and switch on. Add oil gradually through the small feeder tube of the pusher.

6. The small hole at the bottom of the pusher allows the oil to trickle slowly into the bowl. Gradually turn up the speed to MAX.

JUICE EXTRACTOR ·PRESSING ·SQUEEZING

1. Fruit or vegetable juices only take a few seconds with the juice extractor. Refer to the detailed instruction booklet on how to prepare food to be processed using this method. Put the food in the feeder tube.

2. Set the speed to MAX and switch on, pushing down the food with the pusher. Only put in small quantities at a time and clean the filter regularly.

3. You can use the masterpress attachment for making sauces or juices. Set the speed to 3, switch on the processor and put in food.

4. For fruit purées and sauces, turn up the speed right towards the end. Use the appropriate sieve according the food to be processed: refer to the guide table in the instructions.

5. Cut citrus fruits in half. Place one half on the cone, set the speed to MIN and switch on, pressing down firmly. The bowl will hold up to 1 litre of juice.

Please refer to individual recipes for an alternative accessory for purées and sauces, depending on which model you have chosen.

SAUCES

MAYONNAISE

Fit the whisk attachment to the food processor and put in the egg yolk, mustard, salt and pepper. Set the speed to 3 and switch on. Once you have got an even mixture, pour in the oil through the small feeder tube of the pusher (a hole in the bottom allows the oil to trickle in slowly). Gradually increase the speed up to MAX.
Pour in the vinegar right at the end and whisk for a few seconds longer.

To be sure of always getting your mayonnaise just right, take all the ingredients out of the fridge 1 hour before using them to bring them all up to the same temperature.
Mayonnaise does not keep for more than one day, so eat it straight away.

COCKTAIL SAUCE: add 2 tablespoons of ketchup, 1 teaspoon of worcester sauce, 1 teaspoon of cognac and a few drops of tabasco sauce to the mayonnaise.

SAUCE VERTE: add 5 tablespoons of chopped mixed herbs (parsley, chives, tarragon, chervil, etc.).

TARTARE SAUCE: add 1 tablespoon of capers, 4 gherkins, 1 shallot, 1 tablespoon of mixed herbs, all chopped using the metal blade or the mill.

LIGHT MAYONNAISE: add 1 stiffly beaten egg white into the mayonnaise.

1 egg yolk
1 teaspoon mustard,
salt, pepper
200 ml oil
1 teaspoon wine vinegar

AIOLI (GARLIC MAYONNAISE)

Peel the cloves of garlic, put them in the bowl fitted with the metal blade and chop finely on speed 12.
Remove the blade and attach the whisk, then add the egg yolk, salt and pepper and switch on at MIN speed. Pour in the oil through the small feeder tube, turning the speed up to MAX right at the end.

Serve the aioli with cooked vegetables and cod, with fish cooked in stock, on croutons with fish soup, with cold chicken or on cold meats, etc.

SAUCE ROUILLE: chop a small red pepper with the garlic and add a pinch of saffron to the salt and pepper.

2 to 3 cloves garlic
1 egg yolk
salt, pepper
100 ml olive oil
100 ml sunflower seed oil

SAUCES

2 shallots
100 ml vinegar
2 tablespoons chopped tarragon
salt, pepper
2 egg yolks
150 g butter

BEARNAISE SAUCE

Melt the butter slowly in a saucepan. Peel the shallots and chop in mill set to MAX speed. Put them in a small saucepan with 1 tablespoon of tarragon and add the vinegar. Bring to the boil and simmer until you are left with a tablespoon of liquid. Leave to cool for a while then add the egg yolks, 2 tablespoons water, salt and pepper. Mix well and heat over a *bain-marie*. Leave to thicken, stirring all the time. Once thickened, transfer into the bowl and whisk at MIN speed.
Add the butter bit by bit through the feeder tube until the mixture becomes smooth and creamy (2 minutes). Add the rest of the chopped tarragon and whisk for 10 seconds at MAX speed. Heat up over *bain-marie*.

Goes perfectly with grilled meat, grilled, poached or steam-cooked fish, fondue bourguignonne, etc.

GREEN PEPPERCORN BEARNAISE: replace the shallots with 2 tablespoons of ground green peppercorns.

CHORON SAUCE: add 2 pureed tomatoes to the sauce. Goes well with veal grenadin or grilled chicken.

2 egg yolks
1 teaspoon lemon juice
1 teaspoon cold water
salt, pepper
150 g butter

HOLLANDAISE SAUCE

Melt the butter slowly in a saucepan.
Put egg yolks, lemon juice and water in a small saucepan over a *bain-marie* on low heat. Leave to thicken stirring all the time. Add salt and pepper.
Once the sauce has thickened, transfer into the bowl and whisk at MIN speed, adding the melted butter little by little. Once you have a smooth texture, whisk on MAX speed for 10 seconds.
Season to taste and serve.

This sauce goes well with fish terrine or poached fish, asparagus, artichokes, etc.

SAUCE MOUSSELINE: add 50 g of fresh whipped cream to the hollandaise sauce. Reheat stirring continuously. Delicious with asparagus or artichokes!

SAUCE MALTAISE: use orange juice instead of lemon and add blanched orange peel and 1 teaspoon of curaçao. Serve with asparagus.

TOMATO SAUCE

Peel the onion and cloves of garlic. Chop them in the bowl using the metal blade at MAX speed. Put aside.
Put the tomatoes in boiling water before skinning them. Seed and chop coarsely in the processor using the pulse button. Heat the oil in a frying pan and fry the onion and garlic gently until transparent. Add tomatoes, concentrated tomato purée, bouquet garni, salt, pepper and sugar. Stir in and simmer gently uncovered for 30 minutes. Remove the bouquet garni and season to taste before serving.

Add extra flavour to the sauce with parsley, basil or freshly cut tarragon.

BOLOGNAISE SAUCE: add 1 grated carrot, 1 finely chopped stick of celery and fry 200 g of minced beef with the onion before adding the tomatoes.

1 kg ripe tomatoes
1 onion, 2 cloves garlic
2 tablespoons olive oil
1 bouquet garni
(thyme, parsley, bayleaf)
1 tablespoon concentrated
tomato purée
salt, pepper
1 pinch of sugar

TOMATO PUREE

 or

Put the tomatoes for 30 seconds in boiling water and quarter. Fit on the masterpress with the medium-mesh sieve and set speed to 3 (or use the metal blade in the processor bowl). Switch on and put in the tomatoes. Add salt and pepper to the purée to taste. Add oil. Mix well and chill in the fridge.

500 g ripe tomatoes
salt, pepper
1 teaspoon olive oil

SORREL SAUCE

Take sorrel leaves off stalks and clean. Melt in a saucepan with the butter for 2 minutes, add salt and pepper and pour in the cream. Bring to the boil and simmer for 5 minutes. Pour the sauce into the blender and blend at speed 10. Season to taste and heat through if necessary.

Serve this sauce with grilled or poached fish (salmon, John Dory), veal or poultry.

1 bouquet fresh sorrel
10 g butter
salt, pepper
200 ml fresh cream

STARTERS

GRATED CARROTS

SERVES 4

300 g carrots
1 teaspoon mustard
1 teaspoon vinegar
salt, pepper, 3 tablespoons oil
1 tablespoon chopped parsley

Cut the carrots into pieces 6 to 7 cm long and lay them flat in the feeder tube of the processor. Use disk A. Switch on at MAX speed. Season with mustard and parsley vinaigrette.

Halve the amount of oil and add orange juice.
Instead of the mustard, add a pinch of ground cumin and a finely chopped clove of garlic.
Mix carrots with grated apple, use lemon juice instead of vinegar and add some raisins and ground hazelnuts.

BEETROOT SALAD

2 beetroot, 1 small shallot
salt, pepper
1 teaspoon vinegar
1 tablespoon groundnut oil
2 tablespoons sunflower seed oil

Peel beetroot and stand upright in the feeder tube. Slice with disk H. Season with vinaigrette and sprinkle with freshly cut chives.

Can be accompanied by lambs' lettuce, chicory and walnuts, or button mushrooms.

CUCUMBER YOGHURT

1 cucumber, salt, pepper
1 teaspoon vinegar
2 tablespoons olive oil
1 yoghurt, freshly chopped mint

Peel cucumber and stand upright in the feeder tube and cut into round slices with disk D. Season with yoghurt vinaigrette.

For special occasions use cream instead of yoghurt, dill instead of mint and serve with smoked fish (salmon, halibut) marinated in lemon juice and dill.

MUSHROOM AND RADISH SALAD: slice the mushrooms (laid flat in the feeder tube) using disk H and the radishes (stood upright) using disk D. Season with cream (200 g) and lemon (1 tablespoon lemon juice) sauce.

CELERY, APPLE AND WALNUT SALAD, accompanied by mayonnaise.

GREEK SALAD: slice cucumber, onion and pepper using disk H, season with olive oil vinaigrette and eat with fresh feta cheese and olives.

GRUYERE AND SAVELOY SALAD: cut into sticks with the chipping disk and season with vinaigrette.

◁ Mixed salad and cream cheese with herbs.

PÂTÉ DE CAMPAGNE

Cut the cooked ham into thick strips. Cut the other meat into pieces. Put the veal and pork into the processor and mince for 20 seconds using the metal blade on MAX speed. Mince in 4 or 5 short bursts at the end, using the "Pulse" button.

Put the meat aside in a salad bowl and mince the bacon fat for 15 seconds, then mince in 4 or 5 short bursts at the end.

Clean mushrooms and slice with the parsley and peeled shallots for 20 seconds. Fry gently in butter for 5 minutes, then add the minced meat. Stir in the egg, add salt, pepper and nutmeg. Mix well.

Garnish the terrine with alternate layers of filling and strips of ham, saving enough filling to do the top layer. Sprinkle with thyme leaves and put the bayleaf in the middle.

Cover and cook over a bain-marie in a pre-heated oven at 180° C, Gas Mark 6, for 1 1/2 hours. Leave the terrine to cool for at least 15 hours and chill before serving.

CHEESE SOUFFLÉ

Grease the dish with butter. Preheat oven at 200° C, (Gas Mark 6/7). Dice the cheese and chop finely in the processor using the metal blade at MAX speed.

Make a béchamel sauce : melt butter in a saucepan and add flour. Mix until it starts to bubble then add the milk. Cook for 8 to 10 minutes, stirring continuously until the sauce thickens. Season with salt, pepper and nutmeg and mix in the cheese. Remove from heat and add egg yolks one at a time.

Add a pinch of salt to the egg whites and beat in the processor using the whisk. Set the speed to MAX and beat until stiff.

Add to the rest of the mixture.

Pour into the dish and bake for 35 minutes.

Serve hot.

FISH TARTARE

Squeeze the lime. Put the juice in a glass. Put the leaves of the mixed herbs in the bowl. Attach metal blade, set to speed 12 and chop herbs. Cut fish fillets into pieces and chop coarsely in about ten short bursts. Put the fish aside in the fridge.
Remove the metal blade and attach the whisk. Put the egg yolk, salt and pepper into the bowl. Beat at speed 6 then pour in oil through the small feeder tube of the measurer and whip the sauce like a mayonnaise, adding the lime juice while whipping. Stop to pour in the soya sauce and saffron. Whip again for 5 seconds. Mix together the sauce and the fish and mixed herbs.
Season to taste and leave to chill. Serve with a little salad.

As the fish is to be eaten raw, make sure it is perfectly fresh. You can use the same recipe with other fish, like salmon trout, sea bream, fresh cod or haddock.

SERVES 4

180 g filleted sole
180 g filleted salmon
2 sprigs dill
3 sprigs chervil
1 egg yolk, salt, pepper
6 tablespoons olive oil
1/2 teaspooon soya sauce
1 lime, 1 pinch saffron

PREPARATION: 15 min.

* for all models which include this accessory

FISH TERRINE

Tear bread into pieces and put into milk. Chop the lemon peel and dill finely in the mill.
Cut the fish fillets into pieces and mince them in the processor using the metal blade on MAX speed for 20 seconds. Add the soaked bread and mince for a further 10 seconds. Add the eggs, cream, chopped lemon peel and dill, salt and pepper and mix in at speed 6 for 10 seconds.
Melt 10 g of butter in a frying pan and brown the fillet of salmon for 30 seconds on either side on a high heat. Grease the terrine with the butter and pour in half of the fish filling. Lay the salmon fillet on top and cover with the rest of the filling. Cover the terrine and bake in a preheated oven at 180° C, Gas Mark 6, for 15 minutes, then take off the lid and bake for a further 10 minutes.
Drain off any excess liquid towards the end.

* Use whole fish and have them filleted or fillet them yourself.
Pre-filleted fish that have been stored in ice before being purchased release too much water during cooking. Sink a knife into the terrine to see when it is cooked. The knife should come out clean.
Serve hot with lemon butter or sorrel sauce, or cold with herb mayonnaise.
You can also use smoked salmon instead of fresh salmon.

SERVES 6

25 g decrusted white bread
50 ml milk
350 g white fish fillets (dab, sole, whiting, fresh cod, etc.)*
2 large eggs
100 g fresh cream
salt, white pepper
1 180 g salmon fillet
peel of 1/2 lemon
5 sprigs dill
20 g butter

UTENSILS
3/4-litre terrine

PREPARATION: 20 min.
COOKING TIME: 25 min.

STARTERS

PIKE QUENELLES

SERVES 4

400 g pike flesh
2 egg whites
150 g fresh cream

Court-bouillon
1/4 l white wine, 1 carrot
1 onion, 1 clove
1 sprig thyme, 1 shallot
1 bayleaf, 1 sprig parsley
salt, pepper

PREPARATION: 15 min.
COOKING TIME: 20 min.

Cut the pike flesh into pieces and mince for 30 seconds in the processor on MAX speed with the metal blade. Pass the minced flesh through a sieve and put in the fridge.

Prepare the court-bouillon: pour 1/2 litre of hot water into a saucepan and add the wine, sliced carrot, onion studded with the clove, the thyme, bayleaf and parsley tied together in a bouquet, the finely chopped shallot and salt and pepper. Bring to the boil and cook for 15 minutes.

Mix the egg whites one at a time with the pike, stirring well. Add cold cream, salt and pepper and work in. Shape 12 quenelles using 2 tablespoons. Strain the court-bouillon over the saucepan and simmer quenelles in it for about 4 minutes.

Serve with a Nantua or Hollandaise sauce, or with a white butter sauce.

PIZZA

SERVES 4 to 6

300 g dough
1 onion, 1 clove garlic
600 g fresh tomatoes
1 sprig thyme
4 tablespoons olive oil
150 g mozzarella cheese
8 anchovies in oil
16 black olives
salt, pepper, oregano

PREPARATION: 15 min.
COOKING TIME: 30 min.

Make the dough as shown on page 51 (white bread). Leave it to stand for 15 minutes then knead rapidly and roll out into a circle 28 cm in diameter on a baking sheet sprinkled with flour.

Skin and seed the tomatoes and chop them coarsely with the metal blade in 4 or 5 short bursts on MAX speed.

Peel and chop the onion and clove of garlic. Heat up 2 tablespoons of oil in a frying pan and fry the chopped onion and garlic gently for 1 minute, then add tomatoes, thyme, salt and pepper. Cook over a moderate heat until you have a fairly thick pulp.

Slice the mozzarella thinly.

Preheat the oven at 240° C, Gas Mark 8.

Brush the surface of the dough with oil. Spread the tomato pulp over the dough. Garnish with slices of cheese and anchovies (arranged in a star shape) and sprinkle with oregano.

Spread out the olives and pour over a tablespoon of olive oil.

Bake the pizza for 15 to 20 minutes.

You can vary the recipe in a variety of ways by garnishing with saucisson, ham, seafood, artichokes, mushrooms, peppers, onions, capers, etc.

ONION TART

Make the pastry (see page 49) and leave to stand.
Attach disk H in the processor and set to MAX speed.
Peel onions and stand upright in the feeder tube and chop.
Preheat the oven at 210° C, Gas Mark 7. Blanch the onions in boiling water for 5 minutes then drain them. Roll out the pastry in the greased flan dish. Place a circle of greaseproof paper weighed down with dried beans on top and bake for 15 minutes.
Melt the butter and onions in saucepan for 10 minutes, stirring continuously.
Chop the parsley in the mill at MAX speed.
Beat the eggs for 10 seconds in the processor using the whisk at speed 4, then add cream, cream cheese, parsley, salt and pepper and mix for 20 seconds, gradually turning up the speed to 8.
Spread out the onions over the pre-cooked pastry base and pour over the cream.
Turn down the oven to 180° C and bake for 30 to 35 minutes.
Serve hot with a salad.

*Y*ou can also add a few smoked bacon lardons or 70 g of sliced cheese (Comté, for instance).

*T*ry leeks or chicory instead of onions.

SERVES 6

Shortcrust pastry
200 g flour, 100 g butter
salt, 50 ml water

Filling
250 g onions
2 stalks parsley
20 g butter, 3 eggs
150 g fresh cream
175 g low-fat cream cheese
drained in strainer
salt, pepper
2 sprigs parsley

UTENSILS
1   25 cm flan dish

PREPARATION: 20 min.
COOKING TIME: 40 min.

QUICHE LORRAINE

Make the pastry (see page 49) and leave to stand for 30 minutes.
Preheat the oven at 210° C, Gas Mark 7.
Roll out the pastry in the greased dish. Prick the base and pinch down the edges with a fork. Bake for 15 minutes.
Dice the streaky bacon into lardons and fry gently in a frying pan without adding any fat. Leave to drain on a paper towel.
Beat the eggs for 20 seconds in the processor with the plastic blade at speed 4, then stop to add the milk, cream, salt, pepper and a little grated nutmeg. Beat for 20 seconds. Spread out the lardons over the pre-cooked pastry base and pour over the cream. Turn down the oven to 200° C and bake the quiche for 30 minutes.
Serve hot.

*A*s a variation, try half lardons and half stoned prunes.

*F*ill the base with diced ham and crumbled roquefort. Do not add too much salt to the cream.

*U*se strips of ham and blanched peppers instead of lardons.

*O*r button or wild mushrooms, sauteed in butter.

SERVES 6

Shortcrust pastry
200 g flour, 100 g butter
1 pinch salt, 50 ml water

Filling
180 g smoked streaky bacon
150 ml milk, 3 eggs
salt, pepper, nutmeg
180 g fresh cream

UTENSILS
1   25 cm flan dish

PREPARATION: 15 min.
Leave pastry to stand 30 minutes
COOKING TIME: 45 min.

SOUPS

GASPACHO

Peel the cucumber, skin and seed the tomatoes, peel the green pepper, onion and cloves of garlic. Cut all these ingredients into pieces, put them in a salad bowl and add 1/4 litre of very cold water, the vinegar, tabasco, salt and pepper.
Mince the bread for 10 seconds in the blender attachment on MAX speed then pour in half of the contents of the salad bowl and blend until the mixture is smooth (50 seconds). Transfer into a soup tureen and blend the rest of the soup ingredients. Transfer into the soup tureeen and add the olive oil and 1 tablespoon of lemon juice. Mix in, correct seasoning and leave to cool.

You can prepare little dishes of diced cucumber, tomato, onion and pepper (cut into sticks with the chipping disc then dice by hand), mixed herbs and bread cubes to accompany the soup.
The tomatoes will be easier to skin if you scald them in boiling water for 20 seconds.

SERVES 4

1/2 cucumber (280 g)
2 tomatoes (400 g)
1/2 green pepper
1 small mild onion
2 cloves garlic
1/4 litre water
20 g stale bread
1 teaspoon wine vinegar
few drops tabasco sauce (optional)
2 tablespoons olive oil
salt, pepper, 1/2 lemon

PREPARATION: 20 min.

CHILLED YOGHURT SOUP

Peel the carrots. Wash the celery sticks and cut into pieces. Wash the apple and quarter it. Peel the grapefruit and cut into 8.
Put the carrots, celery, apple and grapefruit, in that order, in the juice extractor and transfer the juice into a soup tureen.
Wash and dry the mixed herbs then chop them in the mill or use the metal blade in the processor bowl. Add the herbs, yoghurt, salt and pepper to the juice in the tureen and mix in by hand with a whisk. Leave to chill for 30 minutes before serving.

SERVES 4

500 g carrots
2 sticks celery
1 yellow grapefruit
1 green apple, salt, pepper
2 creamy liquid yoghurts
5 sprigs chives
2 sprigs parsley

PREPARATION: 15 min.

◁ Gaspacho

25

SOUPS

  or

SERVES 4

150 g leeks
100 g onions
200 g potatoes
20 g butter
200 ml milk, 1/2 litre water
salt, pepper, nutmeg
2 nice sprigs of chervil

PREPARATION: 10 min.
COOKING TIME: 30 min.

LEEK AND POTATO SOUP

Peel the leeks and onions. Attach disc H in the processor and set speed to MAX. Stand the vegetables upright in the feeder tube and chop finely. Melt the butter in a saucepan and add the leeks and onions. Stir, cover and cook for 10 minutes.
Peel the potatoes and cut them in half lengthways. Stand them upright in the feeder tube and chop them finely. When the leeks and onions have been cooking for 10 minutes, add the potatoes. Season with salt, pepper and grated nutmeg. Pour the milk with 1/2 litre of hot water into the saucepan.
Cook for a further 20 minutes.
Chop the chervil in the mill or use the metal blade in the processor bowl. Season the soup to taste and sprinkle with mixed herbs.

You can change the flavour of the soup by using parsley, tarragon, basil or other herbs instead of the chervil.

Blend the soup in the blender attachment or the bowl using the metal blade. Add a tablespoon of cream.

SERVES 4

100 g sorrel
130 g potatoes
250 g button mushrooms
25 g butter
600 ml water, salt, pepper
100 g fresh cream

PREPARATION: 10 min.
COOKING TIME: 22 min.

CREAM OF MUSHROOM SOUP WITH SORREL

Peel and wash the vegetables. Cut the potato into pieces and chop for 20 seconds in the processor with the metal blade on MAX speed.
Melt the butter in a saucepan and add the sorrel leaves and the chopped potato. Stir and leave to melt while you chop the mushrooms.
Add the chopped mushrooms to the contents of the saucepan, add salt and pepper and leave to cook for 2 minutes.
Pour in 600 ml of very hot water. Cover and leave to simmer on a low heat for 20 minutes.
When cooked, pour the soup into the blender attachment, set the speed to 12 and blend for 40 seconds. Return the soup to the saucepan, add the cream, correct seasoning, mix in and leave to cook for a further 2 minutes.
Serve hot.

You can also add a few drops of lemon juice at the end.

For a traditional cream of mushroom soup, simply leave out the sorrel.

VEGETABLE SOUP

SERVES 4

Peel and wash all the vegetables (do not peel the courgette). Stand them upright in the feeder tube and slice them using disc H on MAX speed. Melt the butter in a saucepan and add the vegetables. Cook for 4 to 5 minutes on a low heat, stirring continuously. Add salt and pepper and pour in 1 litre of very hot water. Bring to the boil and simmer for 25 minutes.
Chop the parsley in the mill or in the processor bowl using the metal blade and sprinkle over soup just before serving.

Add an extra little touch with a spoon of fresh cream.

MINESTRONE: add tomatoes, green or haricot beans, 1 onion and noodles. Flavour the soup with basil.

2 carrots, 2 turnips
1 small courgette
1 leek
1 potato
1 stick celery
1 clove garlic
20 g butter, salt, pepper
1 litre water
2 sprigs parsley

PREPARATION: 10 min.
COOKING TIME: 30 min.

CREAM OF TOMATO SOUP

SERVES 4

Skin the tomatoes (scald in boiling water for 10 seconds first), seed them and cut them into pieces.
Peel the onion and the clove of garlic and chop them in the mill or in the processor bowl using the metal blade on MAX speed. Heat up the oil in a saucepan, add the onion and garlic and cover and fry for 2 minutes on a low heat. Add the chopped tomatoes, thyme, salt and pepper, mix well and pour in 1/3 litre of boiling water. Leave to cook uncovered for 20 minutes.
Remove the thyme and pour the soup into the blender attachment and blend for 40 seconds on speed 12.
Return the blended soup to the saucepan and add the cream. Heat for 2 minutes, season to taste and sprinkle with chopped basil.

For added flavour put in fresh blanched broad beans with their skins removed (simply press between fingers).

Halve the amount of tomatoes and add carrots or pumpkin.

800 g fresh tomatoes
1 small onion
1 clove of garlic
2 tablespoons olive oil
salt, pepper
1 sprig thyme
2 tablespoons fresh cream
10 basil leaves
1/3 litre water

PREPARATION: 10 min.
COOKING TIME: 25 min.

MAIN DISHES

RED BREAM IN PAPILLOTES

Cut out 4 sheets of greaseproof paper large enough to hold the fillets and their garnish. Preheat the oven at 230° C, Gas Mark 7/8.
Attach disc C in the processor. Peel the carrots.
Wash the courgette but do not peel. Cut the vegetables into pieces 6 to 7 cm long and lay them flat in the large feeder tube and switch on at MAX speed.
First cook the carrots in salted boiling water for 2 minutes.
Grate the courgettes and add to carrots. Cook for a further 2 minutes then drain.
Arrange a little *julienne* of finely chopped vegetables on each sheet of paper, lay the bream fillet on top and cover with vegetables. Add salt and pepper and sprinkle with lightly crushed coriander seeds.
Add a knob of butter on top and squeeze on a little lemon juice.
Wrap the fillets and garnish in their papillotes, put them in an oven dish and bake for 10 minutes. Serve in the papillotes.

SERVES 4

2 carrots (200 g)
2 small courgettes (200 g)
1 lemon, salt, pepper
30 g butter
12 coriander seeds
4 red bream fillets
   (110 g each=two 500 g bream)

UTENSILS
greaseproof paper

PREPARATION: 10 min.
COOKING TIME: 15 min.

BAKED FRESH COD

Peel the shallots and chop them with parsley leaves in the processor using the metal blade on MAX speed for 15 seconds.
Put chopped shallots and parsley in a saucepan, add 10 g of butter, cover and fry gently. Skin and seed the tomatoes and chop them coarsely in the processor in 4 or 5 short bursts. Preheat the oven at 200° C, Gas Mark 6/7.
Add the tomatoes to the shallots. Pour in white wine, add salt and pepper and bring to the boil. Leave to simmer for 15 minutes on a moderate heat then transfer into an oven dish.
Arrange fish slices on top. Sprinkle fish with salt and pepper and bake for 15 minutes in the oven.
Keep the fish warm and pour the juices into the blender attachment, add 50 g of butter cut into pieces and blend for 30 seconds on MAX speed.
Serve sauce with fish.

You may need to heat up the sauce for a few minutes over a very low heat.

Serve with steam-cooked potatoes or rice.

SERVES 4

4 slices fresh cod
   (160 g each)
salt, pepper
400 g fresh tomatoes
2 shallots
3 sprigs parsley
50 ml dry white wine
60 g butter

UTENSILS
1 oven dish

PREPARATION: 10 min.
COOKING TIME: 30 min.

BRANDADE

Leave the dried cod to soak overnight in cold water, changing water regularly.
Put the cod in a saucepan, cover with cold water and add pepper and a bouquet garni of 1 sprig of parsely, 1 sprig of thyme and 1/2 bayleaf. Bring to the boil and cook for 8 minutes.
Heat the milk until lukewarm in one saucepan, and oil in another. Drain cod thoroughly, remove bones and separate fish into pieces.
Peel and finely chop the garlic in the processor with the metal blade.
Put in the cod and mince slowly at speed 4.
Gradually pour in the milk and oil alternately through the small feeder tube until you obtain a creamy purée; add a few drops of lemon juice towards the end and add salt and pepper if required.

Serve with little croutons fried in oil and steam-cooked potatoes.

Put the brandade in an oven dish and bake au gratin.

SERVES 4

500 g salted dried cod
150 ml milk
150 ml olive oil
1 clove garlic, pepper
parsley, thyme, bayleaf
few drops lemon juice

PREPARATION: 10 min.
Soaking time overnight
COOKING TIME: 10 min.

STUFFED TOMATOES

Soak the bread in the milk. Peel the shallots and clove of garlic.
Wash parsley and remove stalks and chop for 15 seconds in the mill or in the processor bowl using the metal blade on MAX speed with the shallots and garlic. Put aside.
Cut the meat into pieces and mince for 20 seconds on MAX speed in the processor using the metal blade. Add the bread, chopped shallots and parsley, salt, pepper, a pinch of grated nutmeg, 1 tablespoon of oil and the egg yolk. Mix quickly in 5 or 6 short bursts. Preheat the oven at 200° C, Gas Mark 6/7.
Cut off the top of the tomatoes to make a lid and spoon out the insides. Chop the pulp coarsely and fill each tomato with stuffing.
Put the stuffed tomatoes in an oven dish, spreading the chopped pulp around the edges, and pour over remaining oil. Leave to cook in the oven for 40 minutes.

Put some pre-cooked rice in the oven dish before baking.

Or add a little pre-cooked rice to the stuffing or use leftovers from a beef stew instead of pork.

SERVES 4

4 large tomatoes
240 g boneless pork loin
60 g fresh bacon fat
20 g decrusted bread
4 sprigs parsley
1 clove garlic
2 shallots
1 egg yolk
salt, pepper, nutmeg
3 tablespoons olive oil
3 tablespoons milk

UTENSILS
1 oven dish (20 cm x 20 cm)

PREPARATION: 15 min.
COOKING TIME: 40 min.

STEAK TARTARE

Cut the meat into pieces just before serving and mince in the processor for 15 to 20 seconds on speed 12, using the metal blade and mincing in short bursts towards the end ("PULSE").
Make 4 meatballs and flatten them out in the middle of each plate. Chop the shallots and parsley. Put half an egg shell on each meatball with a raw egg yolk inside. Arrange little piles of parsley, shallots and capers around the meat.
Each guest may then season to taste with the garnishes on the table.

Serve with chips or sauteed potatoes, lettuce, lentils, butter beans or potato salad.

SERVES 4

700 g lean steak
4 very fresh eggs
4 shallots or small pickling onions
4 tablespoons capers
1 small bouquet parsley

On the table:
mustard, ketchup
Worcester sauce, tabasco sauce,
salt, pepper,
sunflower seed or groundnut oil

PREPARATION: 10 min.

MINCED BEEF WITH MUSTARD

Peel the shallots and wash and dry the parsley. Chop in the processor using the metal blade at speed 12. Cut the meat into pieces and mince at the same speed for 15 to 20 seconds. Mix in the mustard, egg, salt and pepper, working in short bursts. Make 4 steaks and sprinkle lightly with flour. Fry in butter and oil.

WITH PAPRIKA: mix together 600 g of minced meat and 1 onion chopped and fried in butter with 1 tablespoon of paprika and 1 tablespoon of chopped parsley. Add 1 egg, marjoram, salt and pepper. Fry in butter.

MOROCCAN STYLE: mix together 700 g of minced meat (beef or lamb) and 1 small onion, 1 clove of garlic, 20 leaves of fresh coriander, 8 leaves of mint (chopped); pinch of chilli pepper, 1 teaspoon ras-el-hanout (strong spice), 1 teaspoon crushed cumin, salt, pepper and 1 egg. Make meatballs out of the mixture and put on a skewer for grilled or barbecued kebabs.

AMERICAN STYLE: Cook a beef burger in a frying pan. Heat up a small roll for 5 minutes in the oven. Coat both halves with mayonnaise. On the bottom half, put on: cut lettuce, cheese, chopped mild gherkins, chopped onion, ketchup, steak, more cheese and gherkins and sliced tomato. Close to make a sandwich and put in the oven for a further 2 minutes.

SERVES 4

2 shallots
4 sprigs parsley
600 g shoulder of beef (or steak)
3 tablespoons mustard
1 egg, salt, pepper
1 tablespoon flour

PREPARATION: 10 min.
COOKING TIME: 5 to 6 min.

MAIN DISHES

SERVES 4 to 6

1 chicken cut into pieces
  (1 kg 400)
1 large onion, 1 clove garlic
2 tomatoes
2 tablespoons oil
2 heaped teaspoons Madras curry
  powder
cooking salt, pepper
1 pinch cayenne pepper
1 sprig thyme, 1 yoghurt
1/4 litre chicken stock
1 apple

PREPARATION: 10 min.
COOKING TIME: 30 min.

CHICKEN CURRY

Heat the oil in a saucepan and fry the chicken pieces until golden brown. Peel the onion and clove of garlic. Skin and seed the tomatoes. Prepare the spices and heat up the stock.

Chop the onion and garlic in the processor for 15 seconds at MAX speed using the metal blade. Put aside. Chop the tomatoes coarsely in 5 to 6 short bursts. Remove the chicken from the casserole and put in the onion and garlic. Fry for 2 minutes, stirring all the time, and add spices.

Leave to cook for one more minute then add the tomatoes, thyme, yoghurt and hot stock. Return the chicken to the saucepan. Stir, cover and cook for 20 minutes on a moderate heat.

Peel and quarter the apple. Stand quarters upright in the feeder tube and slice on MAX speed using disc H. Add to chicken after it has cooked for 20 minutes and leave to simmer for a further 10 minutes. Serve very hot with rice, grated coconut and chutney.

You can also add other spices: 6 cardamom seeds, 1/2 teaspoon cumin seeds, 1 teaspoon fresh grated ginger, 2 cloves, etc.

Halve the amount of apple and add 1/2 banana.

SERVES 4

400 g chicken or turkey breast
1 shallot, 1 clove garlic
peel of a lime
25 leaves fresh coriander
salt, pepper, 1 egg white
20 g decrusted bread, flour

Sauce
1 low-fat yoghurt
2 tablespoons cut coriander
1 pinch chilli powder
2 tablespoons lime juice

PREPARATION: 15 min.
COOKING TIME: 15 min.

LIME POULTRY CROQUETTES

Peel the shallot and clove of garlic and chop for 1 minute with the lime peel and coriander in the processor on MAX speed using the metal blade.

Add the chicken or turkey breasts cut into pieces and the bread, and mince for 1 minute. Add the egg white, salt and pepper and mix in a few short bursts. Use this mixture to make 8 small croquettes and sprinkle them lightly with flour. Heat the oil in a frying pan and fry the croquettes until browned all over.

Pour the yoghurt into the processor, add the coriander, chilli powder, salt, pepper and lime juice and whisk at speed 10.

Serve the croquettes on a hot plate and the sauce in a sauceboat.

Use parsley instead of fresh coriander.

Serve the croquettes without sauce and with salad, using the lime juice instead of vinegar to make the vinaigrette.

STUFFED CHICKEN

Clean and wash the mushrooms. Wash and dry parsley and remove leaves. Mince the chicken liver, parsley, chopped mushrooms and bread in the processor for 15 seconds on MAX speed
using the metal blade.
Preheat the oven at 220° C, Gas Mark 7. Melt 15 g of butter in a frying pan and fry the stuffing for 2 minutes on a moderate heat. Add salt and pepper and leave to cool.
Once the stuffing has cooled, stuff the chicken and sew it up (or plug with a ball of greaseproof paper).
Put the chicken in an oven dish, coat it with 15 g of butter and put in the oven. Cook for 15 minutes.
Peel and quarter the potatoes. When the chicken has cooked for 15 minutes, arrange the potatoes around it, adding knobs of butter, and leave to cook for a further 35 minutes.

You can of course prepare the chicken without the potatoes. Spinach will go just as well with it.

SERVES 4

1 chicken weighing
  1 kg 400 with liver
200 g button mushrooms
3 stalks parsley
60 g butter
20 g decrusted bread
700 g potatoes (average
  weight 100 g each)
salt, pepper

PREPARATION: 10 min.
COOKING TIME: 50 min.

CHILI CON CARNE

Leave the kidney beans to soak overnight in cold water.
The next day, put them in a large stewpot, cover with water, add 1 teaspoon of cooking salt and cook for 45 minutes.
Peel the onion, cloves of garlic and chillis. Skin and seed the tomatoes. Cut the shoulder of beef and streaky bacon into pieces and mince them in the processor for 10 to 15 seconds using the metal blade on speed 12, finishing off with 4 or 5 short bursts.
Remove the meat, set to MAX speed and chop the onion and garlic, then chop the chillis separately. Prepare the stock (1 cube).
Just before the beans finish cooking, fry the onion, garlic, bacon and minced beef in oil for 3 to 4 minutes. Then add the chillis, tomatoes, oregano, salt and pepper. Leave for a few minutes and pour in the stock, having first mixed in the tomato purée.
Add the drained beans and mix in. Leave to cook for 1 hour, stirring 2 or 3 times. Serve very hot.

You can use 3 tablespoons of chilli sauce instead of the fresh chillis if you wish.

SERVES 8

500 g red kidney beans
1 large onion, 2 cloves garlic
150 g streaky bacon
1 kg shoulder of beef
4 large tomatoes
3 chilli peppers
2 tablespoons oil
1/2 l beef stock
1 teaspoon oregano
cooking salt, pepper
2 tablespoons concentrated
  tomato purée

PREPARATION: 15 min.
Soaking time overnight
COOKING TIME: 1 hour 45 min.

SHEPHERD'S PIE

  or

Peel the potatoes, cut them into pieces and boil them with a pinch of cooking salt.
Chop the cheese in the processor with the metal blade on MAX speed and put aside. Chop the onions, the clove of garlic and the parsley and fry in a covered pan with 15 g of butter. Mince the bacon for 15 seconds and add to previously chopped mixture.
Cook for 4 minutes while you mince the stewed beef.
Mix all these ingredients together and add salt and pepper.
Preheat the oven at 220° C, Gas Mark 7/8.
Attach the masterpress on the processor (or use the plastic chopping blade in the processor bowl) and make a purée, adding the milk while you blend, on speed 3 (as shown on page 37). Add salt, pepper and nutmeg. Add 70 g of butter cut into pieces and mix well. Spread a layer of purée over the bottom of an oven dish, then alternate layers of filling and purée, saving enough purée for the top layer. Sprinkle with gruyère and knobs of butter and bake in the oven for 20 minutes.

You can use minced steak (to be cooked with the onion) instead of stewed beef or even leftovers from a joint of roast beef or cooked guinea-fowl.

Add a few lettuce or spinach leaves when cooking the potatoes.

SERVES 4 to 6

1 kg potatoes
30 g gruyère cheese
2 onions, 1 clove garlic
400 g stewed beef
100 g fresh bacon
salt, pepper, nutmeg
3 stalks parsley
100 g butter
100 ml milk

UTENSILS
1 oven dish (20 x 24 cm)

PREPARATION: 15 min.
COOKING TIME: 30 min.

CALF'S LIVER WITH CHICORY

Chop the parsley in the mill or use the metal blade in the processor bowl. Peel the chicory and stand upright in the large feeder tube of the processor. Chop finely on MAX speed using disc H. Put into a saucepan with 20 g of butter, the lemon juice, salt, pepper and 100 ml of water, cover and melt over a low heat.
Cut the bacon into pieces and mince in the processor for 10 seconds on MAX speed using the metal blade. Then transfer the bacon into a non-stick frying pan (separating with 2 forks) and fry until crispy and golden brown over a moderate heat.
Fry the calf's livers in another pan with 15 g of butter. Add salt and pepper.
Arrange the liver in a large dish, surround with chicory, bacon and parsley sprinkled over the top.

Use cabbage instead of chicory and quarter it before chopping finely. To avoid indigestion, blanch the chopped cabbage for 3 minutes in boiling water before frying in butter.

SERVES 4

700 g chicory
30 g butter
100 g smoked bacon
2 sprigs parsley
2 tablespoons lemon juice
4 slices calf's liver
salt, pepper

PREPARATION: 10 min.
COOKING TIME: 20 min.

VEGETABLES

POTATO PURÉE

Peel the potatoes, cut them into pieces and boil them with a teaspoon of cooking salt. Attach the masterpress to the processor with the wide-mesh sieve.
Once the potatoes are cooked, take them out with a skimming spoon and blend them at speed 3. Add a little cooking water towards the end in order to get the right texture.
Add pepper to the purée, add salt if required and mix in pieces of butter.
(You can also prepare the purée with the metal blade).

POTATOE PURÉE WITH WATER CRESS: add 1/2 bunch of watercress.

CELERIAC PURÉE: cook 1 celeriac with 200 g of potatoes. Use 120 g of cream instead of the butter.

PURÉED PEAS: cook 500 g of shelled peas with 200 g of potatoes. Add 120 g of cream.

 or

SERVES 4

800 g potatoes
1 teaspoon cooking salt, pepper
80 g fresh butter

PREPARATION: 5 min.
COOKING TIME: 15 to 20 min.

CARROT PURÉE

Peel the carrots, cut into pieces and boil them in salted walter.
Reduce into a purée in the masterpress using the medium-mesh sieve.
Add a little cooking water towards the end.
Add salt and pepper and mix in cream.
(You can also prepare the purée with the metal blade).

Add 3 tablespoons of chopped parsley.

 or

SERVES 4

750 g carrots
100 g fresh cream
salt, pepper

PREPARATION: 10 min.
COOKING TIME: 15 min.

SPINACH PURÉE

Peel and wash the vegetables. Cube the potato and put into a stewpot containing 2 l of water and the cooking salt. Bring to the boil, add spinach and cook for 15 minutes. Drain vegetables thoroughly.
Reduce into a purée in the masterpress using the wide-mesh sieve.
Mix the fresh cream and pepper into the purée; add salt if required. Mix well.
(You can also prepare the purée with the metal blade).

If you do not drain the vegetables properly and obtain a very liquid purée, leave to dry out over a low heat.

 or

SERVES 4

1 kg spinach
1 large potato for puréeing (200 g)
1 teaspoon cooking salt, pepper
2 tablespoons fresh cream

PREPARATION: 15 min.
COOKING TIME: 15 min.

SERVES 4

800 g potatoes
200 ml milk
1 small clove garlic
125 g fresh cream
2 egg yolks
salt, pepper, grated nutmeg
30 g gruyère
15 g butter

UTENSILS
1 oven dish (16 x 21 cm)

PREPARATION: 10 min.
COOKING TIME: 50 min.

POTATOES AU GRATIN

Grate the gruyère in the processor on MAX speed with disc A.
Put aside. Turn the disc over onto side D.
Peel and wash the potatoes. Stand them upright in the feeder tube
and slice them.
Preheat the oven at 210° C, Gas Mark 7.
Cut the clove of garlic in half and use it to rub an oven dish, then cut
the rest into thin slices. Arrange the potatoes in the dish with the
slices of garlic. Pour the cream, milk and egg yolks into the
processor and add salt, pepper and a good pinch of grated nutmeg.
Beat with the whisk for 15 seconds on MIN speed.
Pour mixture onto potatoes.
Sprinkle with grated cheese and a few knobs of butter.
Cook for 50 minutes.

Halve the amount of potatoes and add some leeks or celeriac.

*If you have a combined microwave oven, you can cook the dish at
250° C + microwave (power 70%) in 20 minutes.*

SERVES 4 to 6

200 g button mushrooms
750 g courgettes
2 shallots
20 g butter
salt, pepper
180 g fresh cream
3 egg yolks
1 pinch curry powder

UTENSILS
1 oven dish (16 x 21 cm)

PREPARATION: 10 min.
COOKING TIME: 15 min.

COURGETTES AU GRATIN

Wash and dry the courgettes and cut off the tips. Clean the
mushrooms and peel the shallots.
Stand the courgettes upright in the large feeder tube and slice in the
processor on MAX speed using disc H.
Do the same with the onions and shallots, slicing them together.
Melt the butter in a frying pan and fry the shallots and mushrooms
to release their juices for 5 minutes.
Blanch the courgettes in salted boiling water for no more than
5 minutes then drain thoroughly.
Light the oven grill.
Mix the vegetables together and arrange them in an oven dish.
Pour the cream and egg yolks into the processor, add salt, pepper
and curry powder and beat for 30 seconds with the whisk
on speed 6. Pour sauce over the vegetables and cook under the grill
(not too close) for 5 to 7 minutes.

*You can use pieds de mouton or whole meadow mushrooms instead
of the button mushrooms.*

RATATOUILLE

Peel the onion and cut into pieces. Chop for 20 seconds in the processor using the metal blade on MAX speed. Fry the onion gently in 3 tablespoons of oil in a pan over a very low heat.
Attach disc H in the processor. Wash the aubergines and courgettes, do not peel them but cut off the tops. Peel the pepper and cloves of garlic. Stand the vegetables upright in the feeder tube and slice on MAX speed. Add to the contents of the pan with the remaining oil and leave to cook for 15 minutes.
Skin and seed the tomatoes and cut into pieces.
Once the vegetables have cooked for 15 minutes, add the tomatoes with a bouquet of 2 sprigs of parsley, 2 sprigs of thyme and the bayleaf. Add salt and pepper and simmer for 45 to 50 minutes. Slide the lid off to allow excess water to evaporate after 30 minutes.
This way the vegetables will cook in their juices and keep all their taste.

* Use long, thin vegetables that you can put whole into the feeder tube to get nice full slices.

Sprinkle on some cut fresh basil or add black olives before serving.

SERVES 4

1 large onion
5 tablespoons olive oil
400 g small courgettes
250 g aubergines*
600 g tomatoes
 green pepper
2 cloves garlic
thyme, bayleaf, parsley
salt and pepper

PREPARATION: 10 min.
COOKING TIME: 1 hour

VEGETABLE PASTA

Attach disk C to the processor and set to MAX speed. Peel the vegetables (not the courgettes) and slice into 7 cm long pieces. Lay them flat in the lid feeder tube. First grate the leeks and boil them for 3 to 4 minutes in salted water. Drain.
Grate the carrots and blanch for 3 minutes in boiling salted water, then add the grated courgettes and cook for a further 2 minutes. Drain. Cook the pasta in salted boiling water with a tablespoon of oil. Drain once they are « al dente », i.e. still slightly firm when you bite into them. Transfer them into a salad bowl with 20 g of butter and toss. Heat through the vegetables in a saucepan with 20 g of butter and 1 tablespoon of water, then mix in gently with the pasta. Season to taste and serve immediately.

This « vegetable spaghetti » recipe is easy to do and looks very attractive. It goes well with meat and fish.

SERVES 4

1 good-sized leek
2 thin courgettes
3 carrots
salt, pepper
200 g spaghetti
1 tablespoon oil
40 g butter

PREPARATION: 10 min.
COOKING TIME: 10 min.

DESSERTS

STRAWBERRY TERRINE

SERVES 4 to 6

3 tablets of jelly
100 ml water
80 g sugar
200 g fresh or frozen redcurrants
100 g very cold single cream
400 g strawberries

UTENSILS
1 1/2-litre terrine

PREPARATION: 15 min.
Allow for 6 hours before serving
COOKING TIME: 5 min.

Leave the jelly to soak in cold water.
Attach the masterpress on the processor with the fine-mesh sieve.
Pour 100 ml of water with the sugar into a saucepan and bring to the
boil. Simmer for 5 minutes then pour in the redcurrants, leave to
simmer for a minute more then remove from heat. Pour mixture into
the masterpress and blend at speed 3 to obtain a purée or use the
blender. Beat in the drained jelly with a hand whisk. Leave to cool.
Whip the cream in the processor with the whisk until light and fluffy:
start slowly on speed 3 then increase gradually up to 10. Mix in the
whipped cream with the redcurrant purée.
Grease the terrine with butter and pour in a little redcurrant purée
(1 cm). Leave to set for 5 minutes in the freezer compartment.
Cover with a layer of washed strawberries. Pour over another layer
of cream, cover with strawberries and finish with a layer of cream on
top. Tap the sides of the terrine lightly so that all the ingredients are
evenly spaced out and the cream evenly spread.
Cover with the lid and chill for about 6 hours.

*Serve the terrine in slices with a strawberry or pineapple purée.
Decorate with mint leaves.*

RASPBERRY PURÉE

FOR 250 G OF PURÉE

200 g raspberries
50 g castor sugar
1 tablespoon lemon juice

PREPARATION: 5 min.

Quickly wash the raspberries and drain them.
Attach the masterpress on the processor with the medium-mesh
sieve. Switch on at speed 3 and pour in the raspberries, sugar and
lemon juice*. Gradually increase the speed up to 8 right at the end.
* (or use the metal blade in the processor bowl and pass the purée
through a sieve afterwards).

*Goes well with cheesecake or mousse, sponge cake, vanilla ice
cream, Bavarian cream mousse, etc.*

*Follow the same method to make a strawberry purée. For a
redcurrant or blackcurrant purée, heat the berries so that they split
before reducing them into a purée for best results.*

SERVES 4

800 g cooking apples
2 tablespoons lemon juice
1 tablespoon honey
1 pinch powdered cinnamon
  (optional)

PREPARATION: 15 min.
COOKING TIME: 15 min.

Peel the apples, cut into pieces and put in a saucepan. Add honey mixed in with the lemon juice and put on heat.

Cover and cook the apples until soft (approx. 15 minutes or 6 minutes in a microwave at 100%). Leave to cool for a while before reducing them into a compote in the processor using the metal blade on MAX speed.

You can also use the masterpress to make the compote with the medium-mesh sieve or the plastic blade in the processor bowl.

For extra flavour, try mixing 2 or 3 different varieties of apple.

Mix apples with pears or with dried apricots (previously soaked).

Put a little yoghurt or fjord cream cheese in some small dishes, top with apple compote and decorate with raspberries. Sprinkle over a few grilled almonds.

SPICY COMPOTE: Cook the apples with 1 clove, 1 vanilla pod, a pinch of aniseed, powdered ginger and lime peel.

 * or

SERVES 6

1 kg juicy oranges
2 lemons
180 g sugar
8 tablets jelly
450 g strawberries (fresh or frozen)

UTENSILS
1 brioche tin

PREPARATION: 15 min.
Prepare in advance
COOKING TIME: 5 min.

* for all models which include this accessory

STRAWBERRY JELLY

Leave the jelly tablets to soak in cold water.

Squeeze the oranges and lemons: you will need 600 ml of juice. Pour the juice into a saucepan, add sugar and bring to the boil.

Remove from heat and add drained jelly tablets.

Melt them by beating with a hand whisk.

Wash and hull the strawberries. Reduce them into a smooth purée with the masterpress and the fine-mesh sieve on speed 3 (or use the metal blade in the processor bowl and pass the purée through a sieve afterwards). Add orange and lemon juice towards the end.

Leave to cool then pour into the tin. Leave to set overnight in a cool place.

Plunge the tin in hot water before turning the jelly out.

Use pineapple or peaches instead of strawberries.

CHEESECAKE

Preheat the oven at 180° C, Gas Mark 6. Grease the tin with butter and line it with greased greaseproof paper. Pour the cream cheese into the processor, set to speed 6 and blend for 20 seconds using the plastic blade. Continue blending and pour the sugar and eggs in one at a time through the feeder tube.

Stop the processor, mix in the cornflour, the inside of the vanilla pod, the orange peel and fresh cream; blend and pour in the orange juice through the feeder tube. Continue to blend for 15 seconds to obtain a smooth and even mixture.

Wash the processor bowl, replace the blade with the whisk and set speed to MAX. Beat the egg whites until stiff then fold in with the cream in 3 goes.

Pour the mixture into the tin and cook for an hour in the oven. Leave to cool for a while before turning out onto a dish.

Serve the cake well chilled on its own or with slices of fruit or a fruit sauce. This cake is very light as there is no pastry in it.

SERVES 6

350 g well drained cream cheese (in strainer)
125 g sugar
3 eggs
60 g cornflour
1 vanilla pod
200 g fresh double cream
1 teaspoon orange juice
grated peel of 1/2 orange

UTENSILS
1   22 cm sandwich tin

PREPARATION: 15 min.
COOKING TIME: 1 hour

PEACH MOUSSE

Peel 6 peaches, stone them and reduce into a purée in the processor using the metal blade on MAX speed. Add the lemon juice and sugar and blend for a further 10 seconds. Leave to chill.

Wash the processor bowl and replace the blade with the whisk. Pour in the cream and whip until fluffy, starting on speed 4 and increasing gradually up to 12. Fold in with the purée and spoon the mousse into small dishes.

Cut the remaining peach into slices and use to top the mousses. Decorate with a fresh leaf of mint.

You can use the same recipe with strawberries, apricots, nectarines, etc. For a Bavarian mousse, add 3 tablets of jelly to the peach purée.

SERVES 4

7 good-sized ripe peaches
2 tablespoons lemon juice
150 g very cold single cream
50 g sugar

PREPARATION: 10 min.

DESSERTS

SERVES 4 to 6

200 g dark cooking chocolate
30 g butter
4 eggs
40 g sugar
1 tablespoon fresh cream

PREPARATION: 10 min.
COOKING TIME: 5 min.

CHOCOLATE MOUSSE

Break the chocolate into pieces and melt over a bain-marie (or in a microwave) with 2 tablespoons of water. Remove from heat, add knobs of butter and stir to obtain a smooth mixture.
Put the egg yolks and 20 g of sugar in the processor and beat with the whisk for 30 seconds on speed 8. Add the cream and whip for 15 seconds, then lower speed to 4 and pour in the melted chocolate through the feeder tube. Whisk for 20 seconds and put aside.
Clean the processor bowl and beat the egg whites on MAX speed until stiff (add a pinch of salt).
After 50 seconds pour in the rest of the sugar through the feeder tube and whisk for a further 10 seconds. Fold in the beaten egg whites with the chocolate in 3 goes and leave to chill.

Flavour the mousse with a few drops of coffee essence or grated orange peel.
Halve the amount of chocolate and add candied chestnut purée.
Serve the mousse with a light custard, vanilla, coffee or pistachio sauce (pistachio nuts should be finely chopped and mixed in with milk).

SERVES 4

500 g low-fat drained
  cream cheese
70 g very cold fresh double cream
2 tablespoons honey

PREPARATION: 15 min.

CREAM CHEESE MOUSSE

Leave the cream cheese to drain overnight, removing the whey at regular intervals. You should be left with 400 to 450 g after 24 hours.
Blend the very cold cream cheese with the honey using the metal blade on speed 8 for 1 minute, then leave the cheese aside in a cool place.
Replace the blade with the whisk and whip the very cold cream in the processor with 30 g of ice-cold water until fluffy. Start on speed 3 and gradually increase up to 10 after 1 minute.
Mix together the cream cheese and cream and put in the fridge.

Sprinkle the mousse with ground dried fruit or nuts (hazelnuts, walnuts, almonds) or serve with fresh fruit such as clementines, oranges or sliced figs and red fruits, according to season.
Decorate with grilled flaked almonds, candied orange peel and/or fresh mint leaves.
Pour strawberry sauce around the mousse.
Mix in 100 g of fruit purée and 2 tablets of jelly.
Instead of the honey, use sugar and a little grated lemon peel, or sprinkle the mousse with unsugared cocoa.

DESSERTS

SERVES 6 to 8

60 g sugar lumps
75 g melted butter
350 g grapes (chasselas, muscat
  or Italian)
1/2 litre milk
3 good-sized eggs
60 g castor sugar
1 packet vanilla sugar
75 g flour

UTENSILS
1 25 cm flan dish

PREPARATION: 10 min.
COOKING TIME: 45 min.

GRAPE FLAN

Preheat the oven at 200° C, Gas Mark 6/7. Put the sugar lumps in the pie dish with 2 tablespoons of water and cook until you have a golden brown caramel. Remove from heat and turn dish to coat the base with caramel. Leave to set.
Wash, dry and pick grapes off bunch. Spread them evenly over the base of the dish. Bring the milk to the boil.
Using the plastic blade, put the eggs, granulated sugar and vanilla sugar in the processor and blend for 20 seconds on speed 4, add flour, blend for a further 15 seconds then add the melted butter and pour in the milk through the feeder tube. Blend for another 5 seconds.
Pour the mixture over the grapes and bake for 45 minutes.
Serve cool.

You can prepare separate tarts in small individual dishes. You can make 8 tarts by using 400 g of grapes. Bake for 30 minutes.

For a quick recipe you need not make any caramel. In this case, increase the quantity of castor sugar to 75 g.

You can use cherries, plums, prunes, sliced apple, redcurrants, blackcurrants, etc. instead of grapes.

 *

SERVES 4 to 6

900 g kiwi fruit
1/2 lemon
1 juicy orange
40 g castor sugar

UTENSILS
1 ice cream churn

PREPARATION: 15 min.
+ 20 min. for freezing

* for all models which include this accessory

KIWI FRUIT SORBET

Squeeze the half lemon and the orange. Pour the juice into a salad bowl.
Peel the kiwi fruit and reduce into a smooth purée in the masterpress* with the medium-mesh sieve. Add sugar and mix thoroughly then pour mixture into the ice cream churn. Freeze.

* You can also use the blender attachment or the metal blade. Pass the purée through a sieve afterwards if necessary.

Serve the sorbet with thin slices of mango or orange, with a passion fruit purée or with a selection of red fruits when in season.

Eat with biscuits.

CHOCOLATE ICE CREAM

SERVES 6

1/2 litre milk
5 egg yolks
80 g sugar
50 g unsugared cocoa
100 g fresh cream

UTENSILS
1 ice cream churn

PREPARATION: 10 min.
COOKING TIME: 8 min.
20 to 30 min. freezing time

Heat up the milk. Put the egg yolks and sugar in the processor and beat for 30 seconds on speed 6 with the whisk. Pour in a little boiling-hot milk through the feeder tube, beating all the time, then pour in the rest of the milk and blend. Return the mixture to the saucepan and leave to thicken, stirring continuously. Do not allow the cream to boil. Once it coats the back of the spoon it is cooked. Leave to cool for a while then pour the mixture into the processor bowl. Add the cocoa and whip for 20 seconds on speed 12. Add the fresh cream and whip for a further 10 seconds.
Leave the cream to cool before pouring into the ice cream churn for freezing.

VANILLA FLAVOUR: add a vanilla pod to the egg and sugar mixture and leave out the cocoa.

CHICORY FLAVOUR: heat up the milk with 50 g of chicory, bring to the boil then remove from heat and filter the milk before making the cream.

CARAMEL FLAVOUR: make some caramel with 100 g of sugar and add to the milk. Prepare as above, leaving out the cocoa.

YOGHURT ICE CREAM

SERVES 4

1/2 litre natural yoghurt (4 pots)
300 g frozen raspberries
1 tablespoon lemon juice
50 g icing sugar

PREPARATION: 5 min.

Blend the frozen raspberries in the processor with the metal blade on MAX speed for 30 seconds. Add lemon juice, sugar and yoghurt; blend for a further 20 seconds to obtain an even mixture. Serve immediately in glass dishes.

Use other frozen fruit to vary the recipe.

PASTRIES

SHORTCRUST PASTRY

Put the flour in the processor bowl, add the salt and butter cut into pieces. Mix for 10 seconds on speed 4 with the plastic blade, then pour in the water through the feeder tube as you knead.
Knead for 10 seconds on speed 8 to form a ball of pastry. Leave the pastry to stand for 30 minutes in a cool place.
You can cook the pastry on its own if you wish. Either prick the base and pinch down the edges with a fork or place a circle of greaseproof paper weighed down with dry beans to stop it from rising too much.

You can add a spoonful of sugar when preparing a dessert.

SERVES 6 to 8

200 g flour
100 g butter
1 pinch salt
50 ml water

UTENSILS
1   25 to 28 cm baking tin

PREPARATION: 5 min.

LEMON TART

Prepare pastry as shown above. Leave to stand then roll out into the flan case so that it overlaps on the edges*. Bake the pastry blind for 15 minutes at 210° C, Gas Mark 7.
Wash the lemons and grate the peel over the processor bowl.
Squeeze the lemons (you will need 140 g of juice).
Pour the juice into a glass.
Fit the whisk and beat together the eggs, sugar and softened butter for 20 seconds on speed 10, then add the cream and lemon juice and continue beating until smooth.
Remove the tart from the oven and spread the mixture over the pastry base. Bake in the oven for a further 30 minutes.
Leave to cool before turning out.

* Roll the pastry out thin and cut off excess around the edges and use to make a small tart or for decoration.

Decorate the tart with slices of candied lemon in syrup.

As a variation, use limes instead of lemons.

To make a lemon meringue tart, beat two egg whites stiffly with 2 tablespoons of icing sugar. Spread the meringue mixture on top of the baked tart and brown under the grill.

 *

SERVES 6

Pastry
200 g flour
100 g butter
1 pinch salt
50 ml water

Filling
3 untreated lemons
130 g sugar, 3 eggs
50 g softened butter
100 g fresh double cream

UTENSILS
1   25 cm flan case

PREPARATION: 15 min.
COOKING TIME: 45 min.

* for all models which include this accessory

◁ Lemon tart

SERVES 6 to 8

180 g flour
90 g butter (at room temperature)
60 g castor sugar
1 egg
1 pinch salt

UTENSILS
1 28 cm baking tin

PREPARATION: 5 min.

75 g soft butter
90 g icing sugar
1 egg, 150 g flour
30 g ground almonds
1 pinch salt

1 28 cm baking tin

SERVES 6 to 8

Shortcrust or shortbread pastry
  (see above)

Filling
700 g Golden Delicious or Cox's
  apples
1 lemon
2 tablespoons sugar
grated peel of 1 untreated orange

UTENSILS
1 28 cm flan case

PREPARATION: 15 min.
COOKING TIME: 45 min.

SHORTBREAD PASTRY (SABLÉ PASTRY)

Cut the butter into pieces and beat with the sugar for 10 seconds on speed 6 using the plastic kneading blade.
Add the flour, salt and egg, knead for 10 seconds on speed 12, then 5 seconds on MAX speed until the ingredients are well mixed.
Then remove the pastry and shape into a ball. Leave to stand for a few hours. If not, you can use it straight away, allowing for the fact that it will shrink a little in the oven. In this case, make sure it overlaps the edges of the tin.

Flavour with vanilla, orange blossom or cinnamon.

ALMOND SHORTBREAD PASTRY

Work in the butter with the icing sugar and almonds for 10 seconds on speed 6. Add the flour, salt and the egg and beat for 30 seconds increasing the speed to 12.

SHORTBREAD BISCUITS: roll out the pastry (shortbread or almond shortbread) and cut out separate biscuits with a cutter. Bake on a greased tin dusted with flour.

APPLE TART

Preheat the oven at 200° C, Gas Mark 6/7. Roll out the pastry in the flan case. Prick the base and pinch down the edges with a fork and leave to cool in the fridge for 5 to 10 minutes. Bake for 10 minutes.
Quarter, peel and core the apples. Attach disc H in the processor and set to MAX speed.
Lay the quartered apples flat in the large feeder tube and slice. Coat with lemon juice to stop them from going brown.
Remove the pastry from the oven after 10 minutes and fill with a layer of apples (using the least attractive slices). Sprinkle with grated orange peel and a tablespoon of sugar. Arrange the best slices of apple on top in a circle.
Sprinkle with sifted granulated sugar and return the tart to the oven for 30 minutes.
Serve warm or cold with a little fresh cream.

Mix in 1/2 teaspoon of cinnamon with the sugar.

As a variation, use ground almonds instead of orange peel.

WHITE BREAD

Put the flour, yeast and salt* in the processor bowl with the plastic kneading blade. Set to speed 6, turn on for 4 short bursts then with the processor still running, pour in water through the feeder tube and knead for 20 seconds. Increase the speed to 12 and work for 1 minute 15 seconds until the dough is smooth and supple. The dough will soon form a ball; stop the processor twice while kneading to flatten the ball with your hand, then continue kneading.
Leave the dough to stand for 15 minutes on a work surface dusted with flour, then quickly flatten with your hand and shape as you wish into 1 loaf or 6 rolls. Place on a baking sheet dusted with flour, cover with a clean cloth and leave to rise for 40 to 50 minutes in a warm place (22 to 25° C). The dough should rise to twice its original volume, but no more. Preheat the oven at 240° C, Gas Mark 8. Make slits in the bread with a razor blade, then bake for 25 to 30 minutes (20 min. for rolls). Put a glass of water in the oven to help the crust to form.

*T*o make rolls, cut the dough into pieces the size of a large egg and flatten each ball. Fold the 4 sides in towards the middle, like an envelope. Turn the balls over and shape them with your fingers.

*T*owards the end of kneading, mix in coarsely ground shelled half walnuts or crushed olives with the dough.

*B*rush the rolls before baking and sprinkle with poppy or cumin seeds.

FOR 1 LOAF OR 6 ROLLS

250 g high-quality plain flour
1/2 teaspoon salt
1 packet dry baker's yeast (6 g)
160 g warm water (32° C)

PREPARATION: 2 min.
Standing time: 1 h
COOKING TIME: 25 min.

* The yeast must not come into
  contact with the salt.

GINGERBREAD

Pour the milk into a saucepan, add a pinch of salt and bring to the boil. Remove from heat and mix in the honey.
Leave to cool. Preheat the oven at 160° C, Gas Mark 5/6.
Grease a bread tin with the butter and line with greased greaseproof paper. Attach the plastic kneading blade in the processor and pour in the flour and yeast, then add the spices: aniseed, cinnamon, ginger, cloves and coriander seeds crushed with the back of a spoon.
Set to speed 8 and mix ingredients well.
Pour in the milk and honey through the feeder tube.
Continue kneading, gradually increasing the speed up to 12 until you have a smooth and even dough.
Pour into the tin and bake for 1 hour in the oven.
Turn out the gingerbread onto a cooling rack.

FOR 1 LOAF

125 g milk
250 g honey
1 pinch salt, 250 g flour
1 teaspoon baking powder
1/2 teaspoon ground aniseed
6 coriander seeds
1/2 teaspoon ground cinnamon
1/2 teaspoon ground ginger
2 cloves, 20 g butter for bread tin

PREPARATION: 10 min.
COOKING TIME: 1 hour

PASTRIES

Chou pastry
100 ml water
1 pinch salt
40 g butter
1 pinch sugar
80 g flour
2 large or 3 small eggs

Filling
1/4 litre vanilla ice cream

Chocolate sauce
200 g dark cooking chocolate
40 g butter
50 g fresh cream

PREPARATION: 20 min.
COOKING TIME: 20 min.

PROFITEROLES

Chou pastry: put the water, salt, butter cut into pieces and the sugar in a saucepan, bring to the boil and add sifted flour in one go. Mix energetically with a wooden spoon until a ball of dry pastry forms, making sure that it does not stick to the bottom.
Leave to cool. Meanwhile, grease a baking sheet and dust with flour. Preheat the oven at 180° C, Gas Mark 6.
Transfer the pastry into the processor bowl and attach the plastic kneading blade. Set to MAX speed, start mixing and add the eggs through the feeder tube one by one. Work the pastry until smooth. Leave to cool for a while, then pipe out small well-spaced dots with a piping bag (or use 2 teaspoons*). Brush with egg yolk mixed with a drop of water. Put sheet in the oven and bake for 20 minutes, then leave in the oven for a further 5 minutes with the door half open. Leave to cool on a cooling rack.
Sauce: melt the chocolate in a saucepan over a very low heat (or in the microwave) and add the butter and cream. Mix until smooth.
Fill each chou with a scoop of ice cream and arrange on plates. Put on table and pour over hot chocolate sauce.

* (or tablespoons for making large chous)

*F*or a dessert for a special occasion, decorate the plate with thin slices of fruit chosen to go with vanilla and chocolate, i.e. orange, fig, banana, mango, raspberries, kiwi fruit, etc.

*V*ary fillings with pistachio ice cream and chocolate sauce, chocolate ice cream and vanilla custard, fruit mousse and fruit purée.

200 g flour
2 eggs
1/2 litre milk
50 g melted butter

PANCAKE MIXTURE

1. With metal blade: put all the ingredients in the processor bowl and blend on MAX speed to obtain an even mixture.

2. With blender attachment: pour the milk into the blender, switch on and pour in the egg, flour and the melted butter at the end. Leave the mixture to stand for 30 minutes before using.

*Y*ou can add a little sugar (20 g) to the mixture if you wish or flavour it with orange blossom, vanilla essence, kirsch, Grand Marnier, etc.

PASTRIES

TO MAKE 8 WAFFLES

2 large eggs, 60 g sugar
125 g flour
75 g melted butter
200 ml milk
Icing sugar for decoration

UTENSILS
1 waffle iron

PREPARATION: 10 min.
COOKING TIME: 20 min.

WAFFLES

Pour the egg yolks, sugar, flour and melted butter into the processor bowl and mix at MIN speed using the plastic kneading blade. Pour in the milk through the feeder tube and gradually increase speed to 12. Leave mixture to stand for 15 minutes.
Wash the bowl and replace the kneading blade with the whisk, add the egg whites with a pinch of salt and beat until stiff on MAX speed. Fold in to the mixture.
Pour out a little mixture into a hot waffle iron and start cooking waffles, continuing until all the mixture has been used.
Sprinkle with icing sugar before serving.

Serve the waffles with whipped cream, fruit, or chocolate sauce.

125 g flour
1 egg
1 tablespoon oil
1 pinch salt
150 ml milk

BATTER

Pour all the ingredients into the processor bowl (or blender attachment) and blend on MAX speed with the metal blade until the mixture is smooth but not too runny.
Leave the batter to stand for 1 hour in the fridge. You can then use it straight away or fold in a stiffly beaten egg white.

APPLE FRITTERS: peel and slice 700 g of apples, coating the slices in lemon juice. Sprinkle with sugar and leave to soak while the batter is standing in the fridge.
Heat up fresh oil in a deep frying pan, immerse the slices of apple in the batter and fry them 4 by 4.

10 g baker's yeast
100 g flour
150 ml lager

LOW-FAT BATTER

Mix in the yeast with 3 tablespoons of warm water. Pour the flour into the processor bowl, add the yeast and blend on speed 8 using the plastic kneading blade.
Pour in lager through feeder tube little by little.
Leave the batter to stand in a warm place for at least 30 minutes.

PINEAPPLE FRITTERS: immerse pieces of pineapple in the batter and fry for 30 seconds on both sides. Serve with a strawberry purée.

BRIOCHE

Put half of the flour, the butter, sugar and salt in the processor bowl and beat for 10 seconds on speed 6 with the plastic kneading blade. Add the rest of the flour with the yeast, warm milk, the egg and egg yolks. Knead for 20 seconds then increase to MAX speed and beat for 1 minute until a ball of smooth and supple dough forms.
Leave the dough to stand for 1 hour in a bowl covered with a cloth in a warm place (22 to 25° C).
Then work briskly by hand and put into the greased and dusted brioche tin. Cover and leave to rise until the dough has doubled in volume (1 hour).
Preheat the oven at 180° C, Gas Mark 6.
Brush the surface of the brioche with the egg yolk and bake for 30 to 35 minutes.

Mix in 80 g of chocolate chips with the dough and make into 6 small balls to make individual brioches.

250 g sifted flour
1 packet dry baker's yeast
2 tablespoons warm milk
5 g salt, 30 g sugar
1 egg + 2 yolks, 125 g butter
1 egg yolk to brush dough

UTENSILS
1 brioche tin

PREPARATION: 5 min.
Standing time: 1h
COOKING TIME: 35 min.

APPLE CRUMBLE

Peel and cube the apples and put into a saucepan with the lemon juice, 50 g of sugar, cinnamon and 100 ml of water.
Cover and cook for 15 minutes (or 5 minutes in a microwave).
Sift the flour into the processor bowl with the baking powder, 60 g of sugar, the butter cut into pieces and 1 tablespoon of cold water, and mix in short bursts on speed 10 using the plastic blade to obtain a grainy rather than a smooth mixture.
Preheat the oven at 220° C, Gas Mark 7/8.
Pour off the cooking juice from the apples and put apples in an oven dish. Arrange raspberries on top, then cover with crumble mixture. Bake for 30 minutes until the crumble is golden brown.

Apple crumble can be served warm or cold with a little fresh cream. It is also delicious served the next day.

SERVES 4

900 g Golden Delicious apples
110 g sugar
1 pinch ground cinnamon
  (optional)
2 tablespoons lemon juice
100 g flour
50 g softened butter
1 teaspoon baking powder
150 g raspberries

UTENSILS
1 oven dish (16 x 21)

PREPARATION: 10 min.
COOKING TIME: 45 min.

PASTRIES

SERVES 6 to 8

90 g sultanas
50 g currants
50 g candied lemon and orange, peel
125 g softened butter
100 g sugar, 3 eggs
1 packet vanilla sugar
250 g sifted flour
1/2 packet baking powder (5 g)
5 tablespoons milk

UTENSILS
1 bread tin

PREPARATION: 10 min.
COOKING TIME: 1 hour 15 min.

FRUIT CAKE

Preheat the oven at 180° C, Gas Mark 6.
Grease a bread tin with butter and line with greased greaseproof paper.
Chop the candied fruit peel coarsely in the mill in short bursts or use the metal blade in the processor bowl.
Put into a bowl with the currants and sultanas and 1 tablespoon of flour. Mix together and put aside.
Beat the butter and sugars in the processor for 20 seconds on speed 8 using the plastic blade. Continue to beat and put in the eggs one at a time through the feeder tube, then the milk and finally the flour with the baking powder (using a tablespoon). Mix in the fruit in short bursts at first, then for 10 seconds on speed 6.
Put the mixture in the tin and bake for 1 hour 15 minutes.
Turn out onto a cooling rack.

SERVES 6

125 g icing sugar
125 g ground almonds
45 g cornflour
3 eggs, 35 g butter
grated peel of half a lemon

UTENSILS
1 small brioche tin

PREPARATION: 10 min.
COOKING TIME: 30 min.

ALMOND CAKE

Melt the butter and leave to cool. Grease a small brioche tin and dust with flour. Preheat the oven at 180° C, Gas Mark 6.
Put the icing sugar, ground almonds and cornflour in the processor and start mixing with the plastic blade on speed 6, adding 2 eggs and 1 egg white one at a time through the feeder tube.
Beat for 20 seconds then stop to add the lemon peel and the melted butter and mix for 20 seconds.
Put the mixture into the tin, brush with egg yolk and bake in the oven for 35 minutes.
Once the cake is cooked, turn out onto a cooling rack.

Ideal for tea or served with fruit salad.

SERVES 6 to 8

125 g castor sugar
4 eggs
1 vanilla pod
15 g melted butter (optional)
50 g flour
50 g cornflour
50 g flaked almonds

UTENSILS
1 22 cm round cake tin

PREPARATION: 10 min.
COOKING TIME: 30 min.

SPONGE CAKE

Preheat the oven at 180° C, Gas Mark 6. Grease the tin and dust with flour. Cover the base with flaked almonds. Put the egg yolks in the processor bowl, add 110 g of sugar and the inside of the vanilla pod and whip for 45 seconds on speed 6 using the plastic blade. Mix in the butter, then the flour and cornflour in 5 or 6 short bursts, then beat for 10 seconds. Put aside in a salad bowl.

Wash the processor bowl and replace the blade with the whisk. Put in the egg whites with a pinch of salt and beat until stiff on MAX speed, adding 15 g of sugar when halfway through beating. Fold the egg whites lightly into the mixture.

Put the mixture straight into the tin and bake for 30 minutes. Leave to cool a while before turning out.

You can serve this cake with a fruit purée, custard, compote or fruit salad.

As a variation, use grated lemon peel or a few drops of orange blossom water instead of the vanilla pod.

The sponge can be cut in half and filled with jam or fruit mousse.

Bake in a rectangular tin to make a Swiss roll or Yule log.

SERVES 6

200 g dark cooking chocolate
125 g butter
125 g sugar
60 g flour
4 eggs
10 g butter to grease tin

UTENSILS
1 22 cm sandwich tin

PREPARATION: 15 min.
COOKING TIME: 1 hour

CHOCOLATE CAKE

Grease the tin and line with greased greaseproof paper. Preheat the oven at 160° C, Gas Mark 5/6.

Break the chocolate into pieces and melt over a bain marie (or in the microwave) with 2 tablespoons of water. Remove from heat and add knobs of butter and stir until smooth. Leave to cool.

Put the egg yolks in the processor bowl with 100 g of sugar and mix together for 30 seconds on speed 6 using the plastic blade, then add the melted chocolate, blend and mix in the flour in short bursts. Mix well.

Wash the bowl, replace the blade with the whisk and beat the egg whites until stiff at MAX speed. After 50 seconds, add 20 g of sugar and beat for a further 10 seconds. Lightly fold the egg whites into the mixture in three goes.

Pour into the tin and bake for 1 hour. Turn out onto a cooling rack.

This cake can be cut into thin slices to accompany a red fruit salad or vanilla ice cream.

BLACK FOREST GATEAU

SERVES 6 to 8

Gâteau
10 g butter, 4 eggs
100 g castor sugar
1 packet vanilla sugar
75 g flour
25 g cornflour
25 g unsugared cocoa
1 pinch ground cinnamon
1 heaped teaspoon baking powder
3 tablespoons milk

Filling
300 g drained Morello cherries
1 tablespoon kirsch
400 ml single cream
25 g icing sugar
20 g dark chocolate

UTENSILS
1   22 cm sandwich tin

PREPARATION: 15 min.
COOKING TIME: 30 min.

Preheat the oven at 180° C, Gas Mark 6. Grease the tin and dust with flour. Put 4 egg yolks and the sugars into the processor bowl and blend for 30 seconds on speed 12 using the plastic blade. Add the flour, cornflour, cocoa, cinnamon and baking powder. Mix together in 4 or 5 short bursts, then pour in the milk through the feeder tube and mix for 30 seconds on speed 8 to obtain an even mixture.
Wash the bowl, replace the blade with the whisk and beat the egg whites until stiff on MAX speed. Lightly fold the egg whites into the mixture in 3 goes and pour into the tin. Bake for 30 minutes and turn out onto a cooling rack.
Attach disc C in the processor. Stand the chocolate upright in the small feeder tube and process in short bursts on MIN speed to obtain flakes of chocolate*.
Put the cherries in a bowl with the kirsch and stir.
Whip the very cold cream with the whisk until fluffy. Whip for 30 seconds on speed 3 then increase gradually up to 8. Mix in the icing sugar towards the end.
Once cooled, cut the cake into 3 layers. Spread the first layer with half of the cherries and a third of the cream filling. Put the second layer on top and spread with the remaining cherries and a third of the filling. Put on third layer and spread with the remaining filling. Sprinkle with chocolate flakes.

* Do this in several goes as the chocolate tends to melt.

CURRANT BISCUITS

FOR 45 to 50 BISCUITS

100 g softened butter
125 g icing sugar
2 whole eggs
150 g sifted flour
75 g currants

PREPARATION: 10 min.
COOKING TIME: 10 min.

Put the butter and sugar in the processor bowl and mix until smooth on speed 6 using the plastic blade. Add the eggs, then the flour. Blend until the mixture has an even consistency.
Preheat the oven at 200° C, Gas Mark 6/7. Grease a baking sheet and use a piping bag or 2 teaspoons to space out small drops of the mixture. Top each drop with 4 to 5 currants. Put the sheet in the oven and bake for about ten minutes. The biscuits should be golden around the edges but still light in the middle.
Remove the biscuits using a metal spatula and leave to cool on a rack in several lots.
You can halve the quantities used if you wish.

DRINKS

RISING SUN

Wash the tomato, carrots and the apple. Peel and remove the pith from the orange. Cut the vegetables and fruit into pieces and blend in the juice extractor on MAX speed, feeding them in through the feeder tube with the pusher.
Serve well chilled and decorate with a twist of lime.

TO MAKE 1 GLASS

1 tomato, 2 carrots
1 apple, 1/2 orange

VITAMIN COCKTAIL

Attach the juice extractor on the processor and set to MAX speed or use the blender attachment. Feed in the redcurrants and pieces of apple through the feeder tube with the pusher.
Pour the juice into a glass and sugar with treacle.

TO MAKE 1 GLASS

100 g redcurrants (fresh or frozen)
2 apples
1 tablespoon treacle

CITRUS FRUIT COCKTAIL

Put 2 ice cubes in the processor bowl.
Squeeze the fruits then pour the juice into a glass with the gin. Add grenadine and decorate with a twist of lime and a stalk of mint.
For a cocktail without alcohol, simply leave out the gin.

 *

TO MAKE 1 GLASS

1 orange, 1/2 lemon
1/2 grapefruit
1 dash grenadine
50 ml gin

* for all models which include this accessory

PLANTER'S TEA

Squeeze the oranges and lemons.
Make 1 litre of strong tea and strain it.
Heat up the fruit juice with the rum, then serve in glasses. Add the tea, sugar to taste and decorate with a twist of orange.

 *

POUR 6 PERSONNES

3 oranges, 2 lemons
200 ml rum
1 litre water
4 teaspoons Ceylon tea

* for all models which include this accessory

DRINKS

SERVES 4

5 juicy oranges
1/2 lemon
1/4 litre of bitter orange

* for all models which include this accessory

BITTER ORANGE CUP

Squeeze 3 oranges.
Peel and remove pith from the 2 remaining oranges and the half a lemon and cut into thin slices. Put the slices in a punch bowl or a large jug. Pour in the orange juice and bitter orange. Stir and serve well chilled.

TO MAKE 1 GLASS

1 apple
1 lemon
2 tablespoons honey

* for all models which include this accessory

HONEY APPLE JUICE

Squeeze the lemon. Peel and core the apple, cut into pieces and put into the blender attachment with the lemon juice.
Blend and add 200 ml of hot water with the honey. Blend again to mix well.
Serve hot or cold with ice cubes.

SERVES 4

1 scoop strawberry ice cream
100 g strawberries
1/2 litre well chilled milk

STRAWBERRY MILKSHAKE

Put all the ingredients into the blender attachment and blend for 40 seconds on speed 12.
Serve immediately.

SERVES 4

1 scoop vanilla ice cream
1 vanilla pod
1/2 litre milk

VANILLA MILKSHAKE

Scrape out the inside of the vanilla pod with a knife and mix in with the milk.
Pour the milk and ice cream into the blender and blend for 40 seconds.

As a variation, add 1/2 banana.

APPETIZERS

GUACAMOLE

Peel the onion and the chilli and cut into pieces. Wash and pick off the coriander leaves. Put into the processor bowl and chop for 40 seconds on speed 12 with the metal blade. Peel and remove stones from the avocados.
Skin and seed the tomato, cut into pieces and put into the bowl with the flesh of the avocados and the lemon juice. Add salt and pepper and blend for 40 seconds. Halfway through, stop the processor and scrape round the edge of the bowl with the plastic spatula so that the mixture is in the middle.

Guacamole is traditionally served with sweetcorn galettes that you can buy from delicatessens. You can also serve it with small pieces of toast or raw vegetables.

SERVES 4 to 6

1 small onion
1 tomato
salt, pepper
1 small hot chilli pepper
2 well ripened avocados
1 tablespoon lemon juice
2 sprigs fresh coriander
 (25 leaves)

PREPARATION: 10 min.

CHEESE BISCUITS

Grate the cheese in the processor with disc A. Put the flour, grated cheese and the butter cut into pieces in the processor bowl fitted with the plastic blade.
Add salt, pepper and grated nutmeg. Start kneading on speed 6. Gradually increase speed up to 12 until a ball of dough forms. Leave to stand for 30 minutes before rolling out and cutting into varied shapes with a cutter.
Bake the biscuits in the oven for 10 minutes at 210° C, Gas Mark 7.

150 g comté or emmenthal cheese
150 g flour
150 g soft butter
1 pinch nutmeg
salt, pepper

PRAWN BUTTER

Reduce the prawns into a purée in the processor using the metal blade on speed 8. Add the butter cut into pieces with the lemon juice. Blend until smooth.
Serve on grilled canapés.

50 g shelled prawns
50 g butter
a few drops lemon juice

TAPENADE

Put the olives, anchovies, capers and lemon juice in the processor bowl and blend for 10 seconds on MAX speed using the metal blade before pouring in the oil through the small feeder tube of the measurer. Blend until all the oil has been mixed in. Serve on pieces of toast.

100 g black olives, pitted
100 g anchovies in oil
50 g capers
100 ml olive oil
juice of 1 lemon

INDEX

Imprimé en France   **Aubin Imprimeur**
LIGUGÉ, POITIERS